TABLE OF CONTENTS

CHAPTER 1

SOARING GIANTS

A condor sits high on a rocky cliff. The bird spreads its massive wings. Then it leaps off the cliff. It flies through the air.

Condors sometimes have trouble taking off. They may jump off cliffs to start flying.

The condor circles high above a field. It spots a group of smaller **scavengers** below. They are eating a dead deer.

FAR FLIGHTS

Condors are very heavy. So, they use **currents** of warm air to help them fly. They can glide for 100 miles (160 km) without flapping their wings.

Condors can fly up to 18,000 feet (5,500 m) in the air.

The condor swoops down. It scares the other animals away. Then it begins to eat. Its beak tears into the deer's skin. The large bird gulps down chunks of meat.

FAST FACT

Sometimes, condors eat so much that they can't fly for a while.

Condors can eat more than 15 pounds (7 kg) of meat in one meal.

CHAPTER 2

Condors are some of the largest birds in the world. They can weigh more than 30 pounds (14 kg). There are two **species** of condors.

Male condors are bigger than females.

California condors live on the west coast of the United States and Mexico. Their wings can stretch 9.5 feet (2.9 m).

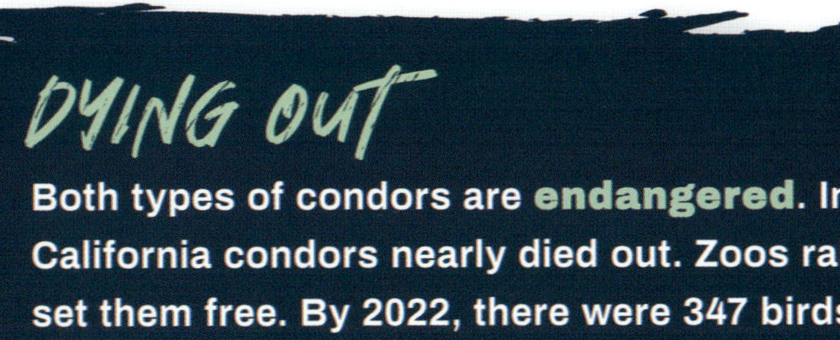

DYING OUT

Both types of condors are **endangered**. In the 1970s, California condors nearly died out. Zoos raised chicks and set them free. By 2022, there were 347 birds in the wild.

California condors are mostly black, but they have white patches on their wings.

Andean condors live along the Andes Mountains in South America. Their wings can stretch up to 10.5 feet (3.2 m).

Andean condors have white feathers around their necks.

CHAPTER 3

SCAVENGERS

Condors are scavengers. They eat dead animals. Condors often eat cows, sheep, and deer. But they will eat smaller animals, too.

Condors sometimes eat in groups. Up to 40 birds may eat the same animal.

Condors may fly 200 miles (320 km) in one day to find food.

Condors have keen eyesight. They can spot dead animals from high in the air. Every day, condors spend hours searching for food.

FAST FACT

Condors can go more than a week without finding food.

After they find food, condors may keep watch for days. Then they fly down to eat. Condors have bald heads. The lack of feathers helps them stay clean while eating.

STRONG STOMACHS

Dead animals often have **bacteria** in them. Condors have **acid** in their stomachs. It keeps them from getting sick. It also helps them break down bones.

Condors help keep nature clean by eating dead animals.

CHAPTER 4

LIFE CYCLE

Condors rest and sleep in groups. They **roost** on cliffs and high tree branches. This can keep eggs and young condors safe from **predators** on the ground.

Scientists often attach tags to condor wings. That helps them track and study the birds.

Female condors lay one egg every one to two years. Parents take turns sitting on the egg. It hatches after two months.

Most condors nest in caves or on cliffs. But some nest in large trees.

Baby condors eat food that their parents spit up.

CONDOR CROPS

A condor has a pouch in its neck called a crop. It can hold up to 3 pounds (1.4 kg) of food. Condors can store the food in their crops for later. Or they can feed the food to their babies.

FAST FACT

Chicks learn to fly after about six months.

Young condors stay with their parents for about two years.

Chicks have brown feathers. The feathers change colors when birds become adults. That happens after six to eight years. Scientists think condors can live 50 years or more.

Each year, scientists release more California condors into the wild.

COMPREHENSION QUESTIONS

Write your answers on a separate piece of paper.

1. Write a few sentences that describe how condors find food.

2. Are you more interested in California condors or Andean condors? Why?

3. How many eggs do condors lay at a time?

   A. one
   B. two
   C. six

4. What would happen if a condor's head was covered in lots of feathers?

   A. The bird would be too heavy to fly.
   B. Bits of food would get stuck in the feathers.
   C. The bird's head would stay cleaner while eating.

5. What does **glide** mean in this book?

*So, they use currents of warm air to help them fly. They can **glide** for 100 miles (160 km) without flapping their wings.*

- A. watch from far away
- B. move smoothly and easily
- C. fall to the ground

6. What does **keen** mean in this book?

*Condors have **keen** eyesight. They can spot dead animals from high in the air.*

- A. loud
- B. weak
- C. strong

Answer key on page 32.

GLOSSARY

acid

A strong chemical that can break down things placed in it.

bacteria

Tiny living things.

combs

Flaps of skin on some birds' heads.

currents

Streams of air that move in a clear direction.

endangered

In danger of dying out forever.

predators

Animals that hunt and eat other animals.

roost

To rest or sleep.

scavengers

Animals that eat dead animals they did not kill.

species

Groups of animals or plants that are similar and can breed with one another.

TO LEARN MORE

BOOKS

Duhig, Holly. *Bones and Bodies*. Minneapolis: Lerner Publications, 2020.

Stuckey, Rachel. *Bringing Back the California Condor.* New York: Crabtree Publishing, 2020.

Wilson, Libby. *Bizarre Birds*. Mendota Heights, MN: Apex Editions, 2024.

ONLINE RESOURCES

Visit **www.apexeditions.com** to find links and resources related to this title.

ABOUT THE AUTHOR

Marissa Kirkman is a writer and editor who lives in Illinois. She enjoys reading about animals, science, and history.

INDEX

ANSWER KEY:
1. Answers will vary; 2. Answers will vary; 3. A; 4. B; 5. B; 6. C